FROM CONFLICT TO COLLABORATION

The Future of Construction Contracts in the Middle East

Saneen M. Sainudeen

TABLE OF CONTENTS

PREFACE

The construction industry in the Middle East has historically operated under traditional, adversarial contract frameworks. While these methods once offered a sense of security through risk-shifting, they have often come at a high cost—escalating disputes, inefficiencies, and financial challenges for contractors. With the construction landscape growing more complex and competitive, there is a clear need to adopt a more collaborative, transparent approach that benefits all stakeholders.

This e-book, From Conflict to Collaboration: The Future of Contracts in the Construction Industry, is a guide for professionals, contractors, and clients looking to navigate the changing dynamics of construction contracting in the Middle East. Drawing on real-world case studies, industry insights, and best practices, this book presents an in-depth examination of collaborative contracts, risk-sharing frameworks, and the principles of trust and transparency in project delivery.

My aim in writing this e-book is to encourage an industry-wide shift toward contract models that prioritize long-term partnerships, efficiency, and sustainable project outcomes. It is an invitation for all stakeholders to consider the transformative potential of collaborative contracts - not only for individual project success but for the future resilience of the construction industry as a whole. I hope this book serves as a valuable resource for professionals committed to building a more robust, efficient, and equitable construction landscape in the region.

Chapter 1: Breaking Free from Adversarial Contracts

For decades, the construction industry has operated under traditional contract models that prioritize risk-shifting over collaboration. The fundamental belief behind these adversarial contracts is that one party can protect its interests by pushing risks onto the other. However, this approach often leads to inefficient outcomes, inflated costs, and unnecessary disputes that undermine project success.

The times have evolved, and if we don't adapt, we risk being left behind. The Human Factor is essential in this transition: it requires readiness to embrace change, the ability to adopt fresh perspectives, the empathy to understand differing viewpoints, and the willingness to share successes with others. For those accustomed to a certain business approach over decades, these shifts can be challenging, yet they are vital for sustained growth and relevance.

The Problem with Traditional Contracts

In the traditional form of construction contracts, such as FIDIC or other widely used standard forms, clients often transfer risk to contractors without fully considering whether the contractor is in the best position to manage those risks.

For example, contractors might be held responsible for unforeseen site conditions, design errors, or delays that are outside of their control. An all-too-familiar statement comes to mind: "It's not my problem; it's in your contract." If we put ourselves in the other party's shoes for a moment, we will definitely see things differently and even act differently. But we choose not to for several reasons.

This creates an atmosphere of confrontation from the start, as each party seeks to minimize its own exposure rather than working toward the mutual success of the project. The consequences are all too familiar:

• **Frequent disputes:** When contracts are adversarial, disputes become inevitable. Each party is more likely to look for opportunities to claim compensation for any perceived breach of contract, which drags projects into lengthy, costly disputes.

• **Project delays:** Disputes can lead to standstills, as projects get bogged down in arbitration, mediation, or worse, litigation. This delays delivery and often increases project costs.

• **Ineffciencies:** In an adversarial setup, parties are more focused on avoiding blame rather than finding solutions to problems as they arise. This can result in missed opportunities for cost savings and effciency improvements.

The Changing Landscape

Fortunately, there is growing recognition across the construction industry, particularly in regions like the UAE, that this adversarial approach is unsustainable. Project complexity, rising costs, and shrinking profit margins are forcing stakeholders to look for more effcient ways of doing business.

Certain fundamental traits, like self- interest, while not inherently negative, often fall short in generating sustainable outcomes. By contrast, qualities like sharing and empathy foster resilience and create lasting impacts in relationships.

Businesses need to embrace a more human-centered approach, as, ultimately, all of our efforts are designed to serve humanity.

More businesses are realizing that a successful project isn't about winning a contractual battle - it's about partnership. They are seeking to replace conflict with collaboration, embracing contracts that foster mutual success rather than confrontation. The shift from risk-shifting to risk-sharing represents the next evolution in contract management, and it is already proving successful in many global markets.

Why Change is Necessary

The construction industry faces unique challenges that make collaboration essential for success:

1. Increasing Project Complexity: As projects become larger and more technically challenging, it is no longer feasible for one party to shoulder all the risk. Collaboration allows for risk-sharing, where each party takes responsibility for the aspects of the project they are best equipped to handle.

2. Financial Pressures: Contractors, consultants, and clients are all under increasing pressure to deliver projects on time and within budget. When disputes arise, they can quickly derail financial forecasts and lead to significant losses for all parties.

3. Global Competition: The construction industry is becoming more competitive, with international firms entering the market. To remain competitive, regional firms must adopt practices that improve effciency and reduce costs. Partnered contracts offer a clear advantage in this respect.

Challenging the Status Quo

Breaking free from the adversarial contract model requires a fundamental shift in mindset.

Stakeholders must move away from a win-lose mentality and embrace the idea that everyone benefits from a project that runs smoothly, is completed on time, and within budget.

But how can this be achieved? It starts with the contracts themselves. Rather than designing agreements that focus on protecting one party at the expense of the other, contracts should be built on the principles of collaboration, fairness, and transparency.

• Fair Risk Allocation: Risks should be allocated to the party that is in the best position to manage them. This not only reduces disputes but also ensures that projects are delivered more effciently and at a lower cost.

• Open Communication: Collaborative contracts foster a culture of open communication between all parties, enabling issues to be addressed early and resolved before they escalate.

• Shared Goals: Contracts should be designed to align the interests of all parties, ensuring that everyone is working toward the same goal -successful project completion.

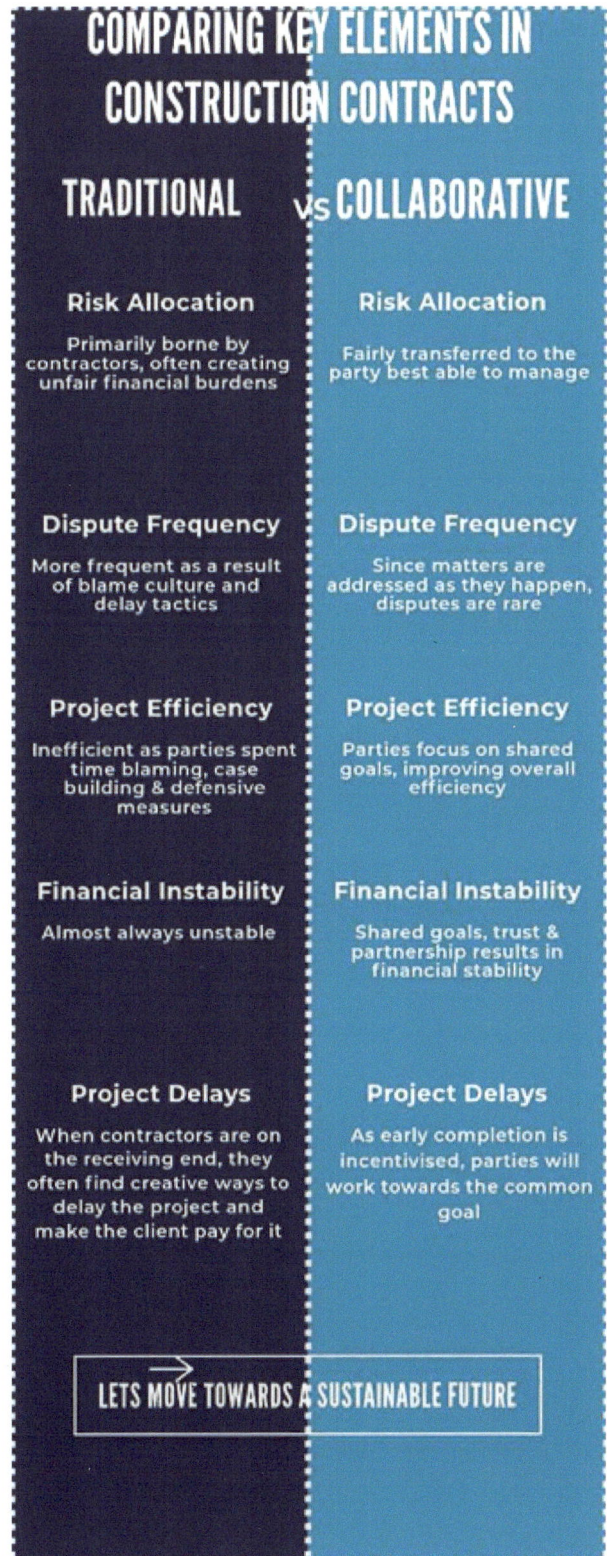

COMPARING KEY ELEMENTS IN CONSTRUCTION CONTRACTS

TRADITIONAL vs COLLABORATIVE

TRADITIONAL	COLLABORATIVE
Risk Allocation	**Risk Allocation**
Primarily borne by contractors, often creating unfair financial burdens	Fairly transferred to the party best able to manage
Dispute Frequency	**Dispute Frequency**
More frequent as a result of blame culture and delay tactics	Since matters are addressed as they happen, disputes are rare
Project Efficiency	**Project Efficiency**
Inefficient as parties spent time blaming, case building & defensive measures	Parties focus on shared goals, improving overall efficiency
Financial Instability	**Financial Instability**
Almost always unstable	Shared goals, trust & partnership results in financial stability
Project Delays	**Project Delays**
When contractors are on the receiving end, they often find creative ways to delay the project and make the client pay for it	As early completion is incentivised, parties will work towards the common goal

LETS MOVE TOWARDS A SUSTAINABLE FUTURE

Conclusion: A New Way Forward

The construction industry is at a turning point. Breaking free from adversarial contracts is no longer just an option; it is a necessity. As the industry evolves, so too must the frameworks that govern it. By challenging the status quo and embracing contract models that prioritize collaboration over conflict, stakeholders can ensure more successful, efficient, and profitable projects.

In the chapters that follow, we will explore the principles of partnered contracts, examine how trust and communication can transform project outcomes, and discuss practical steps for achieving balanced risk allocation and building long-term relationships in the industry.

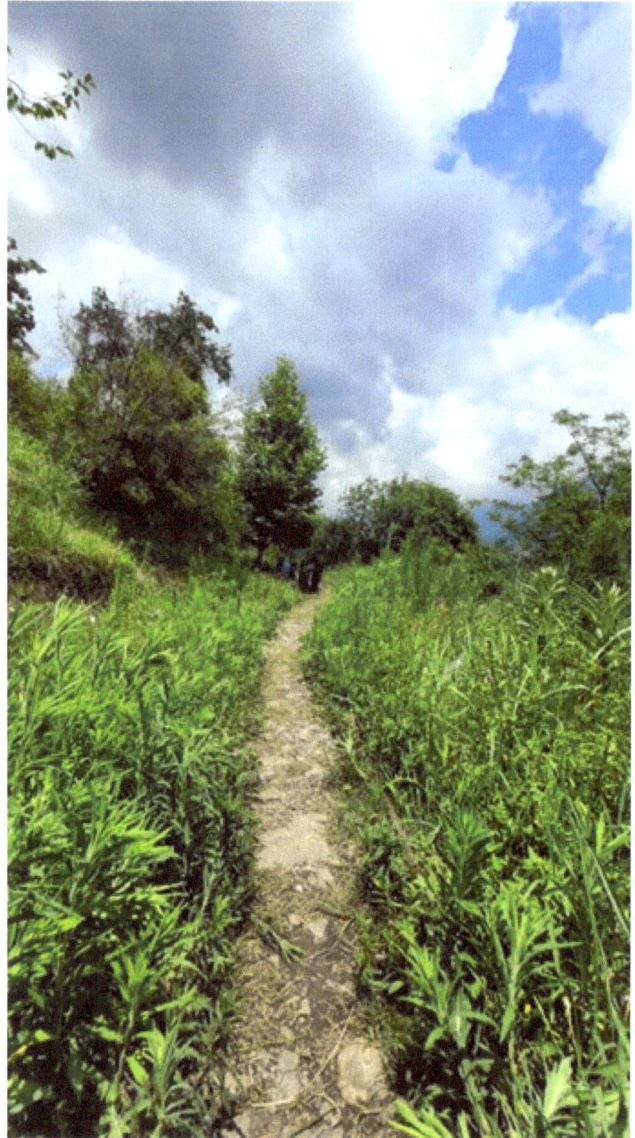

Chapter 2: The Rise of Partnered Contracts

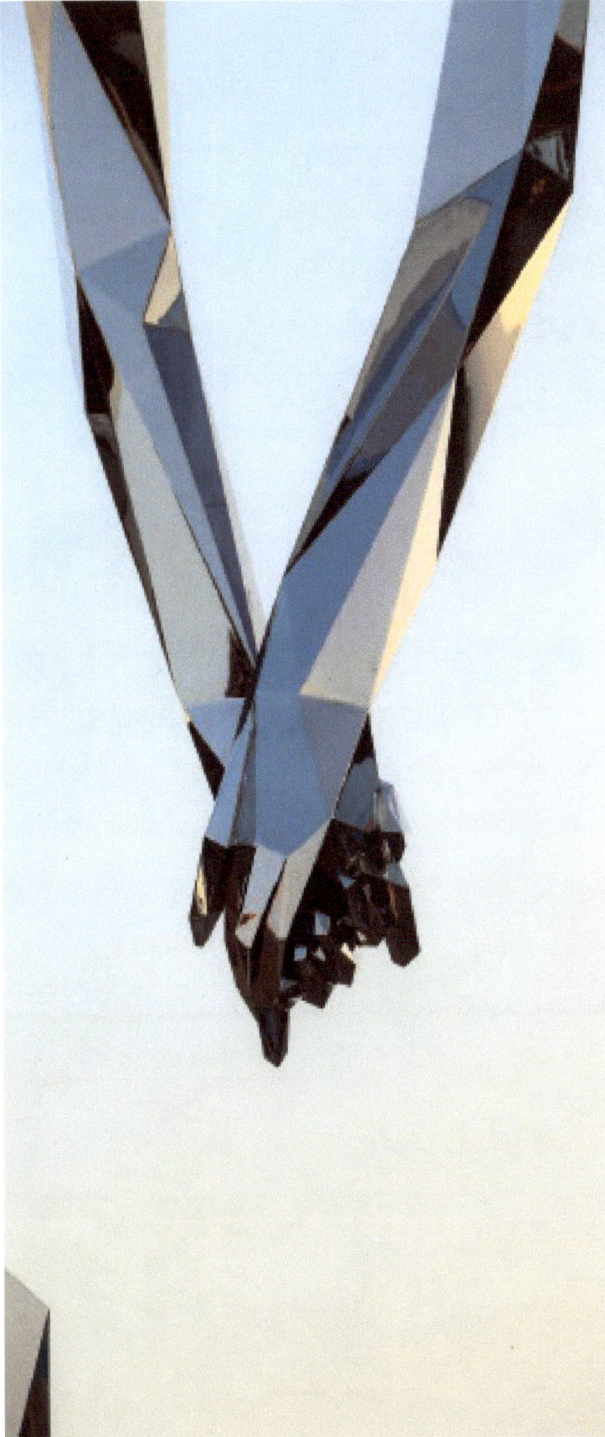

The traditional adversarial approach to contracting in the construction industry has caused inefficiencies, disputes, and escalating costs for decades. Now, a new approach is gaining momentum - partnered contracts. These agreements aim to shift the focus from individual interests to shared goals, creating a more collaborative environment where all stakeholders work toward mutual success.

What Are Partnered Contracts?

Partnered contracts, sometimes referred to as collaborative or relational contracts, differ significantly from traditional forms. Instead of emphasizing risk-shifting, they focus on risk-sharing and open communication. These agreements align the interests of all parties - clients, contractors, consultants, and other stakeholders so that everyone works toward the successful delivery of the project.

Key principles of partnered contracts include:

• Shared Risk and Reward: All parties agree to share both risks and rewards, fostering a more cooperative and problem-solving mindset.

• Transparency: Open communication and transparency in both project progress and financials are required, reducing the chances of disputes.

• Joint Decision-Making: Important decisions are made collectively by all stakeholders, ensuring that the best interests of the project are always prioritized.

• Mutual Trust and Respect: By working together as partners, parties build trust, which leads to more effective collaboration and fewer conflicts.

Benefits of Partnered Contracts

Incorporating partnered contracts into construction projects has demonstrated several key benefits:

1. Fewer Disputes: When parties share risks and rewards, disputes become less frequent. Stakeholders are incentivized to work together to resolve issues early before they escalate into major problems.

2. Increased Efficiency: Partnered contracts promote problem-solving and flexibility, which allows for more efficient project management. Teams can make quicker decisions without the fear of litigation or disputes hanging over every issue.

3. Better Financial Outcomes: Because projects are completed more efficiently, and disputes are minimized, costs are kept under control. Moreover, shared incentives mean that all parties benefit financially from the success of the project.

4. Improved Relationships: Partnered contracts foster long-term relationships rather than transactional, one-off projects. As trust builds over time, stakeholders are more likely to collaborate on future projects, creating a network of reliable partners.

Examples of Successful Partnered Contracts

To start, I want to clarify that my objective is not to advocate for any particular contract template. I encourage each of you to conduct your own research and select the approach that best suits your needs.

My goal is to broaden the industry's perspective, encouraging a deeper exploration of alternative options that promote a more collaborative approach to contracting.

Several global markets have already seen the success of partnered contracts. For instance, in the UK, NEC contracts (New Engineering Contracts) have been adopted to promote collaboration, resulting in fewer disputes and more timely project completions.

Similarly, Integrated Project Delivery (IPD) contracts used in the US combine the efforts of all stakeholders into a single team with shared goals, aligning interests to produce superior project outcomes.

These frameworks are adaptable and can be customized to suit the specific

These frameworks are adaptable and can be customized to suit the speciffc needs of any construction project, regardless of size or complexity. By promoting collaboration, they help create a more harmonious and efficient project environment, ultimately improving the bottom line for all involved.

Challenges to Adoption

Despite the clear benefits, adopting partnered contracts in the construction industry, especially in regions where traditional contracts are deeply entrenched, can be challenging. Here are a few common obstacles:

1. Cultural Resistance: Many construction professionals have spent their entire careers working within adversarial contract frameworks. Moving to a partnered approach requires a change in mindset, which can be diffcult for some to embrace.

2. Lack of Familiarity: In regions like the Middle East, partnered contracts are less common, and stakeholders may be unfamiliar with how they work. Educating clients, contractors, and consultants on the benefits and mechanics of collaborative contracting is crucial.

Educating clients, contractors, and consultants on the benefits and mechanics of collaborative contracting is crucial.

3. Trust Issues: Collaboration hinges on trust, which may be lacking in industries where relationships have historically been adversarial. Building trust between parties takes time, and it may require early wins on smaller projects before larger projects can adopt a partnered approach.

The continuous exit of contractors is indeed concerning. However, many family-owned businesses with decades-long track records offer stability and resilience. Perhaps these firms provide a strong foundation to build upon, given their proven commitment and adaptability in the industry.

How to Introduce and Standardize Partnered Contracts

Introducing partnered contracts to the construction industry requires a concerted effort by all stakeholders. Here are some practical steps:

1. Pilot Projects: Start with pilot projects where all parties agree to use a partnered contract. Focus on smaller projects with less complexity, allowing stakeholders to get comfortable with the new approach.

2. Education and Training: Provide training on how partnered contracts work and the benefits they offer. Workshops and seminars can be effective ways to familiarize industry professionals with collaborative frameworks.

3. Government and Regulatory Support: In many regions, including the UAE, government bodies can play a key role in promoting partnered contracts by mandating their use on public projects. This sets a precedent for private-sector projects to follow.

4. Incentives: Offer financial or reputational incentives to contractors and consultants who embrace partnered contracts. For example, awards for collaborative practices or better payment terms for completing projects under partnered agreements can encourage wider adoption.

Conclusion: The Future of Contracts Lies in Partnership

The construction industry is evolving. As the demand for more efficient, cost-effective, and dispute-free project management grows, partnered contracts offer a clear solution. By shifting from an adversarial mindset to one focused on collaboration and shared success, the industry can move toward a more sustainable, prosperous future.

In the next chapter, we will explore the importance of trust and transparent communication as the bedrock of successful collaborative projects.

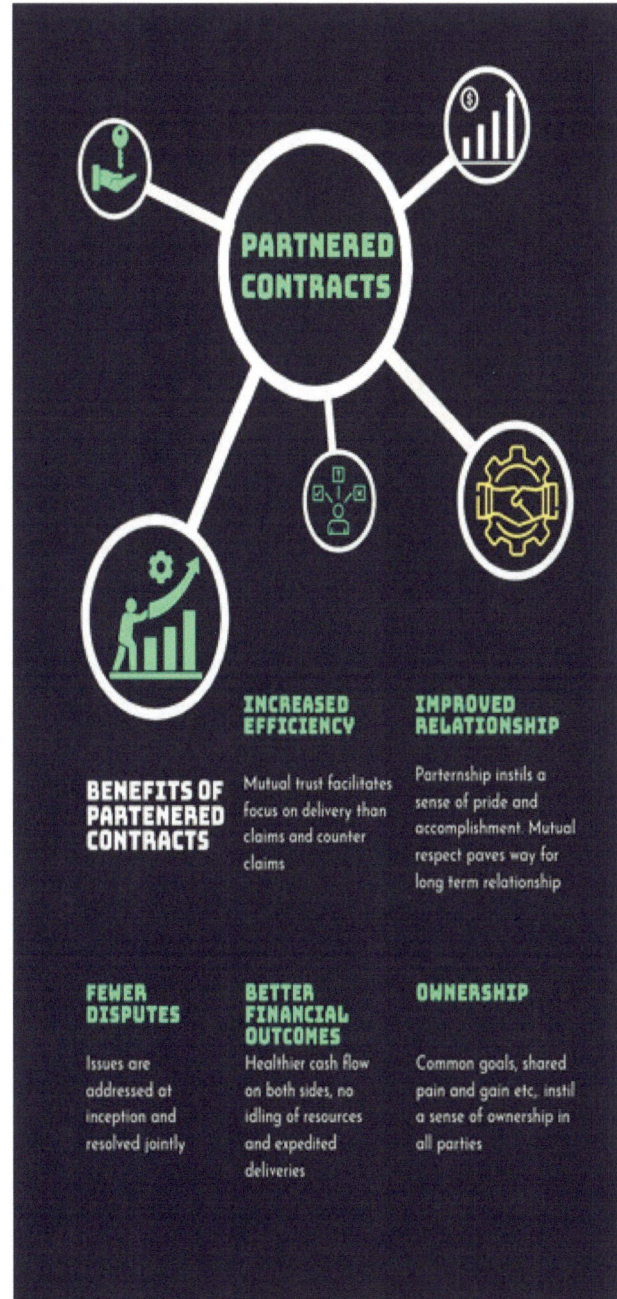

PARTNERED CONTRACTS

BENEFITS OF PARTENERED CONTRACTS

INCREASED EFFICIENCY

Mutual trust facilitates focus on delivery than claims and counter claims

IMPROVED RELATIONSHIP

Parternship instils a sense of pride and accomplishment. Mutual respect paves way for long term relationship

FEWER DISPUTES

Issues are addressed at inception and resolved jointly

BETTER FINANCIAL OUTCOMES

Healthier cash flow on both sides, no idling of resources and expedited deliveries

OWNERSHIP

Common goals, shared pain and gain etc, instil a sense of ownership in all parties

Chapter 3: The Role of Trust and Transparent Communication

At the core of any successful collaborative contract is trust. Without trust, no matter how well-intentioned the contract, collaboration can quickly break down into conflict. In the construction industry, where projects are often complex, large-scale, and require the coordination of multiple stakeholders, trust and transparent communication are essential to overcoming challenges, minimizing disputes, and ensuring successful project completion.

The Importance of Trust

Trust is often cited as the single most important factor in successful collaborations. It is the glue that holds relationships together, particularly in high-stakes industries like construction, where unforeseen issues are almost inevitable. When trust is absent, parties are more likely to resort to defensive, self-serving actions that ultimately harm the project.

are more likely to resort to defensive, self-serving actions that ultimately harm the project.

Case Study: The Success of the London 2012 Olympic Park

In the construction of the London 2012 Olympic Park, trust played a pivotal role. The Olympic Delivery Authority (ODA) implemented NEC contracts (New Engineering Contracts) to foster collaboration between contractors, consultants, and clients. One of the key elements was the open-book approach, which allowed all parties to see the financials transparently.

This transparency built trust between stakeholders and enabled them to work collaboratively toward the common goal of delivering the park on time and within budget. As a result, the project was completed ahead of schedule and £1 billion under budget, demonstrating the power of trust in driving successful project outcomes.

How to Build Trust in Construction Projects

Building trust doesn't happen overnight. It requires deliberate effort and ongoing commitment. Here are several practical steps to foster trust in construction contracts:

1. Open-Book Accounting: As seen in the London Olympics case, sharing financial information creates a culture of transparency, allowing all parties to feel secure that they are receiving fair compensation and that no one is hiding critical financial data.

2. Early Contractor Involvement (ECI): Bringing contractors into the project during the planning stages fosters a collaborative environment from the start. This practice allows contractors to contribute their expertise early on and helps avoid adversarial relationships down the line.

3. Joint Risk Management: Instead of pushing risk onto one party, collaborative contracts encourage stakeholders to work together to identify, manage, and mitigate risks. This shared responsibility for risk fosters a sense of teamwork and mutual respect.

4. Clear Communication Protocols: Establishing clear, structured lines of communication from the beginning of the project helps prevent misunderstandings and disputes.

Regular meetings, real-time progress reports, and digital tools that allow for immediate feedback can improve communication.

The Role of Transparent Communication

Trust cannot exist without transparent communication. In construction projects, where timelines are tight and budgets are fixed, clear and transparent communication is crucial for addressing issues before they escalate into conflicts. When communication breaks down, so does the relationship, often resulting in costly delays or even legal disputes.

Case Study: Heathrow Terminal 5

In a post-project review, stakeholders emphasized the importance of maintaining open lines of communication throughout the project's duration. This transparency allowed for immediate resolution of potential issues before they turned into major setbacks.

Challenges to transparent communication

While the benefits of trust and transparency are clear, achieving these ideals is not always straightforward.

Construction projects often involve multiple parties with competing interests, and communication can easily break down. Some common challenges include:

1. Cultural Differences: In large projects, stakeholders may come from different cultural backgrounds, each with its own approach to communication and problem-solving. Understanding and bridging these cultural gaps is critical for successful collaboration.

2. Technology Gaps: Not all stakeholders may be comfortable with digital tools designed to facilitate communication, which can lead to uneven adoption and information silos. The construction of Heathrow Terminal 5 offers another valuable lesson in the importance of transparent communication. The project adopted a collaborative framework, with contractors and clients working together under a non-adversarial, no-claims approach. By fostering an environment of transparency, of Heathrow Terminal 5 offers another valuable lesson in the importance of transparent communication. The project adopted a collaborative framework, with contractors and clients working together under a non-adversarial, no-claims approach. By fostering an environment of transparency, the project avoided the major disputes that plagued previous UK construction projects of similar scale.

3. Fear of Admitting Fault: In an adversarial contract culture, stakeholders may be reluctant to admit when mistakes are made, fearing financial or reputational damage. A collaborative framework must emphasize that early reporting of issues is not a sign of weakness but a proactive step in ensuring project success.

Steps to Ensure transparent communication

1. Set Communication Standards: From the beginning, it's essential to set clear communication protocols, including reporting structures, frequency of meetings, and communication tools to be used. Everyone should be on the same page.

2. Use Technology Wisely: Digital tools such as project management software or

collaboration platforms (e.g., Procore, Aconex) can streamline communication, enabling all stakeholders to access real-time data and updates. These tools should be user-friendly and accessible to all.

3. Encourage a 'No Blame' Culture: For true transparency to occur, stakeholders must feel safe in reporting issues without fear of retribution. This requires creating a culture of problem-solving rather than fault-finding.

Lencioni's Pyramid - A Model for Teamwork

Lencioni's Pyramid is a teamwork model developed by Patrick Lencioni, presented in his book The Five Dysfunctions of a Team. It outlines five key behaviors that are essential for building cohesive and high-functioning teams:

Trust – At the foundation, trust enables team members to feel safe being vulnerable with each other. Without trust, collaboration suffers as people hold back their thoughts and concerns.

Conflict – Healthy teams engage in constructive conflict around ideas. This level of engagement allows team members to challenge each other and debate options openly, leading to better decision-making.

Commitment – Once ideas are debated, teams can achieve true commitment, where everyone, regardless of personal opinion, aligns with the group's final decisions.

Accountability – Teams that are committed can hold each other accountable for agreed-upon actions and standards, reinforcing mutual responsibility.

Results – At the top, when all prior levels are solid, teams focus on collective outcomes rather than individual achievements, driving superior results.

This model highlights how each layer builds on the previous one to create a resilient and successful team.

You can explore this model further in The Five Dysfunctions of a Team by Patrick Lencioni.

The Five Behaviors® Model

Source https://internalchange.com/patrick-lencionis-pyramid-model/

+Trust one another
+Engage in conflict around ideas
+Commit to decisions
+Hold one another accountable
+Focus on achieving collective results

Conclusion: Building Trust and Transparency for Long-Term Success

Trust and transparent communication are essential foundations of any successful construction project, particularly under collaborative contract frameworks. By focusing on building strong relationships, fostering open communication, and using tools that ensure transparency, the construction industry can achieve better project outcomes.

In the next chapter, we will explore the concept of risk allocation, how it affects the financial health of contractors, and how a more balanced approach can lead to more sustainable project management practices. Also, from here on, case studies will focus specifically on the Middle East, providing readers with relatable, region-specific insights and examples.

Chapter 4: Balancing Risk for a Healthier Industry

In the construction industry, particularly in the Middle East, risk is often unfairly allocated in traditional contracts, with much of the burden falling on contractors. This approach leads to inflated costs, inefficiencies, and, in many cases, the financial instability of contractors. Large-scale projects in the UAE, Saudi Arabia, and other GCC countries have seen major contractors face liquidation or pull out of the market due to unsustainable risk allocation practices. A collaborative, risk-sharing approach is not only fairer but also leads to better outcomes for all stakeholders.

The Consequences of Unfair Risk Allocation

In traditional adversarial contracts, clients tend to shift the majority of risks - such as delays, unforeseen site conditions, and changes in scope, onto contractors. This risk-shifting can have dire consequences, including:

• Financial Strain: Contractors are often forced to inflate their bids to cover the added risk, leading to higher project costs. When risks materialize, it can severely impact their cash flow and financial stability.

• Project Delays: When contractors bear the full brunt of risk, they may adopt overly cautious approaches, which can slow down decision-making and project execution.

• Market Exit of Contractors: As a result of unsustainable risk exposure, many contractors in the Middle East have faced financial distress, leading to high- profile liquidations and exits from the market. This has reduced competition, leaving developers with fewer qualified contractors to choose from.

Case Study: The Construction Crisis in Saudi Arabia (2015-2017)

Between 2015 and 2017, the construction industry in Saudi Arabia saw multiple high-profile contractors, including Saudi Oger and Saudi Binladin Group, face severe financial challenges.

One of the primary reasons cited was the disproportionate risk they bore under traditional contract structures. In a market where delays in payments and unforeseen changes to project scope were common, contractors were often left to absorb the financial impact, leading to insolvency.

This crisis highlighted the dangers of unfair risk allocation and underscored the need for a more balanced, sustainable approach. Since then, the Saudi government and many private developers have taken steps toward more collaborative contract structures that distribute risk more equitably between parties.

The Benefits of Balanced Risk Allocation

Balancing risk fairly between clients and contractors leads to healthier financial outcomes for both parties and improves the likelihood of project success. When risk is distributed according to the party best positioned to manage it, the industry as a whole becomes more resilient and projects are completed more efficiently.

Case Study: The Dubai Expo 2020

In the lead-up to Dubai Expo 2020, the UAE government and developers recognized the importance of balancing risk fairly to ensure project completion on time and within budget. For example, the Expo 2020 contracts adopted more collaborative frameworks, with some projects following FIDIC contract models that incorporated fair risk-sharing clauses.

This approach helped to prevent disputes and delays, allowing contractors to focus on efficient project delivery rather than protecting themselves from disproportionate risk.

As a result, the Expo sites were largely completed on time, even despite the challenges posed by the COVID-19 pandemic. HKA's CRUX Insight report and industry analysis by McKinsey also highlight these collaborative efforts, suggesting lessons learned from Dubai Expo's efficient dispute management and project completion strategies.

Sustainability and waste management practices further lowered potential long-term costs by repurposing 80% of the site post-event, an approach that added financial resilience to the project's legacy phase.

Project Timelines and Risk Management: The infrastructure for Expo 2020, developed over seven years, exemplifies effective project and risk management on a large scale. The joint venture between Mace and Jacobs implemented collaborative practices that ensured seamless project delivery across complex phases—from initial ground preparation to pavilion construction and final testing of event operations.

Dispute Reduction: Expo 2020 adopted NEC contracts, which emphasize collaboration and proactive dispute resolution, making arbitration and mediation easier for contractors. This choice effectively minimized disputes by setting clear guidelines for early issue identification and resolution, which was vital given the event's extensive international scope and the need for real-time problem-solving between stakeholders.

Financial Impact and Legacy Planning: The Expo's investment of AED 5 billion in contracts dedicated to small and medium-sized enterprises (SMEs) was part of a broader risk-sharing and economic inclusivity initiative.

Key Principles of Balanced Risk Allocation

To achieve more sustainable project management and financial health across the construction industry, stakeholders must adopt contract frameworks that distribute risk fairly. Here are some key principles to follow:

1. Allocate Risk to the Party Best Able to Manage It: If a contractor has more control over certain project elements, such as labor or construction methodology, they should bear the associated risks. Conversely, clients should assume risks related to project scope changes or regulatory delays.

2. Use Collaborative Contract Models: Contracts like FIDIC or NEC have built-in mechanisms that promote fair risk- sharing. For example, FIDIC's 2017 edition emphasizes a more collaborative approach, including balanced risk allocation between clients and contractors.

3. Include Provisions for Unforeseen Conditions: One of the most common causes of disputes in the Middle East construction industry is unforeseen site conditions, such as difficult ground or regulatory changes. Including contractual provisions that outline how such risks will be managed, rather than assigning them to one party, can reduce disputes and financial strain.

4. Early Risk Identification and Management: Collaborative contracts encourage early identification and joint management of risks. By identifying potential issues early, the project team can work together to develop mitigation strategies that prevent risks from materializing into costly problems.

5. Establish a Dispute Resolution Mechanism: While fair risk allocation reduces the likelihood of disputes, it's important to have a structured mechanism in place for resolving any conflicts that do arise. Collaborative contracts typically include provisions for mediation or arbitration, allowing for faster, more cost-effective resolutions than traditional litigation.

The Role of Financial Health in a Sustainable Industry

One of the most significant advantages of balanced risk allocation is its impact on the financial health of contractors. When contractors are forced to bear too much risk, they are often unable to maintain the necessary cash flow to stay solvent, particularly on long-term projects.

Case Study: Aldar Properties' Approach in Abu Dhabi

Aldar Properties, one of the leading developers in Abu Dhabi, has been a pioneer in adopting more balanced risk- sharing contracts.

In recent years, Aldar has moved away from contracts that disproportionately place risks on contractors, opting for models that distribute risks more evenly between stakeholders. By doing so, Aldar has helped ensure that contractors remain financially stable, reducing the chances of project delays due to insolvency.

This approach has led to the successful completion of large-scale projects, including Yas Island developments, where contractors worked in a more collaborative and less financially pressured environment.

Several studies have concluded that projects with risk-sharing frameworks report fewer delays and cost overruns.

The "CRUX Insight Report" by HKA might offer some relevant stats on Middle Eastern projects as it explores dispute trends and impacts.

An extract from their report providing some statistical data on the Middle East is provided here under:

Middle East
Regional summary

Number of projects	Number of countries	Average CAPEX value (USD)	Average EOT claimed*	Average cost claimed**
410	12	1.61 bn	82.0%	35.1%

Top claims or dispute causes	Middle East	Rest of World
Change in scope	57.3%	33.3%
Design information was issued late	34.9%	18.8%
Contract interpretation issues	28.8%	17.1%
Design was incomplete	30.5%	19.0%
Contract management and/or administration failure	25.6%	17.7%
Approvals were late	27.1%	11.8%
Cash flow and payment issues	26.6%	11.5%
Access to site/workface was restricted and/or late	25.4%	15.7%
Poor management of sub-contractor/supplier and/or their interfaces	20.0%	19.3%
Design was incorrect	20.0%	23.9%

*% of planned duration **% of CAPEX

>< CRUX

Source: https://www.hka.com/crux-insight-sixth-annual-report- forewarned-is -forearmed/

21

Clearly there are financial advantages of risk-sharing models over traditional contracts. Allow me to provide some insights into insurance premiums, project timelines, and overall cost efficiency:

1. Insurance Premiums

Traditional Contracts: These contracts generally lead to high insurance premiums for contractors, as the bulk of risks—such as design errors, unforeseen conditions, and regulatory delays—are shifted onto them. To mitigate these risks, contractors often need comprehensive coverage, raising premiums by approximately 20-30% depending on project complexity and location

Risk-Sharing Models: In collaborative or risk-sharing contracts, where risks are allocated to the parties best suited to manage them, insurance premiums are generally lower. With clear and fair risk allocation, insurers perceive less exposure, often reducing premiums by 15-20%. This reduction is attributed to minimized claims and smoother resolution protocols, which lower insurers' costs.

2. Project Timelines and Delay Costs

Traditional Contracts: Traditional models often lead to lengthy delays, as issues like unforeseen site conditions or design changes trigger dispute resolution processes. Delays from disputes can extend timelines by 10- 15% on average, depending on the contract's rigidity and the complexity of the issues. This translates into costly downtime and additional financing costs, as well as the risk of liquidated damages.

Risk-Sharing Models: Collaborative contracts focus on early issue identification and open communication channels, which lead to faster resolutions and a smoother workflow. These approaches typically reduce project timelines by 10-20%, especially on complex infrastructure projects, thanks to streamlined decision-making and fewer disruptions from disputes.

3. Financial Illustration

Traditional Contract:
Total Contract Value: AED 500 million
Insurance Premiums: +20% due to high-risk exposure (AED 100 million)
Delay Costs: +15% due to prolonged disputes (AED 75 million)

Total Project Cost: AED 675 million

Risk-Sharing Contract:
Total Contract Value: AED 500 million
Insurance Premiums: +15% due to shared risk (AED 75 million)
Delay Costs: +5% due to collaborative approach (AED 25 million)
Total Project Cost: AED 600 million

In this scenario, the risk-sharing approach yields a 10% overall cost reduction, translating to AED 75 million saved on insurance and delay-related expenses. This illustrates how collaborative contracting aligns with financial resilience by reducing both premiums and potential delay costs.

Conclusion: A Path Toward Sustainable Project Management

The construction industry in the Middle East is undergoing a transformation. Traditional adversarial contracts that unfairly shift risk onto contractors are being replaced by more balanced, collaborative models that promote sustainability and long-term success.

Balanced risk allocation is not just about fairness; it's about ensuring the financial health of contractors and the efficient, dispute-free delivery of projects. By adopting these principles, the industry can move toward a more resilient future, where contractors, clients, and consultants alike share in both the risks and the rewards.

In the next chapter, we will explore how long-term relationships built on trust and collaboration can enhance project outcomes and ensure sustainable growth in the construction industry.

Chapter 5: Building Long-Term Relationships, Not Short-Term Gains

The construction industry in the Middle East has long been driven by a project-centric approach, where each contract is treated as an isolated, one-time transaction. This focus on short-term project gains often comes at the cost of building lasting relationships with clients, contractors, consultants, and other stakeholders. However, as the industry evolves, it's becoming increasingly clear that long-term partnerships built on trust, collaboration, and mutual success are key to creating sustainable growth and delivering better project outcomes.

Why Long-Term Relationships Matter

Long-term relationships in the construction industry offer several clear benefits for all parties involved:

• **Consistency and Efficiency:** Working with trusted partners on multiple projects can lead to smoother project execution. Teams that have worked together before understand each other's expectations, communication styles, and workflows, reducing the learning curve and the potential for miscommunication.

• Cost Savings: Repeat collaborations between clients and contractors can lead to reduced costs over time. Contractors who understand a client's needs are better positioned to provide accurate cost estimates and avoid the pitfalls of under- or over-bidding.

• Risk Reduction: Long-term relationships foster trust, which enables more effective risk-sharing and problem-solving. When parties are committed to working together beyond a single project, they are more likely to seek amicable solutions to challenges rather than resorting to disputes.

• Future Opportunities: Building strong relationships on current projects opens the door to future opportunities. A contractor who delivers a project successfully and fosters a collaborative atmosphere is more likely to be invited back for future projects, ensuring a steady stream of work.

Steps to Foster Long-Term Relationships

While the benefits of long-term relationships are clear, building and maintaining them requires effort and commitment from all parties. Here are some key strategies for fostering lasting partnerships in the construction industry:

1. Prioritize Collaboration Over Profit: In the short term, it might be tempting to maximize profits by focusing solely on project success. However, companies that invest in collaboration and transparent communication with their partners often reap greater rewards over the long run. Prioritizing mutual success leads to stronger partnerships and increased trust.

2. Deliver on Promises: The foundation of any long-term relationship is reliability. Contractors, clients, and consultants need to consistently deliver on their promises—whether related to project timelines, quality, or budget. This consistency builds a reputation of trustworthiness, which encourages future collaborations.

3. Invest in Problem-Solving Together: Issues will arise in any construction project, but the way stakeholders address these issues determines whether the relationship will endure. Rather than pointing fingers, long-term partners should focus on working together to find solutions, ensuring that challenges are viewed as shared problems to be resolved collectively.

4. Promote Continuous Improvement: Long-term relationships can stagnate if partners fail to innovate or improve. To keep the partnership fresh and valuable, parties should continuously look for ways to improve efficiency, reduce costs, and enhance communication.

5. Fair and Open Contracting Practices: Contracts should reflect a commitment to collaboration, with clauses that incentivize long-term partnership rather than short-term gain. Including performance-based incentives, shared savings agreements, or penalty reductions for ongoing partners can reinforce a commitment to the relationship.

The Role of Trust in Long-Term Partnerships

At the heart of every successful long-term relationship is trust. Without trust, even the most promising partnerships can falter. When trust is established, however, parties can engage more openly, share information more freely, and work toward common goals without fear of being taken advantage of.

In the Middle East, partnerships between contractors and government entities are essential for delivering large-scale infrastructure projects efficiently. These collaborations highlight the benefits of transparent communication, risk-sharing, and flexible contracting approaches, allowing projects to stay on track even when unexpected challenges arise. Such partnerships serve as a model for balancing regulatory requirements with contractor capacity.

By working in close alignment, government bodies and contractors can navigate complexities, from regulatory compliance to cost management, creating a sustainable approach that promotes long-term infrastructure goals.

This approach has been successful in many regional projects, such as city-wide transit networks, energy facilities, and smart city initiatives, where contractors and government authorities share the common goal of delivering impactful projects for the region.

Building a Collaborative Ecosystem

For long-term relationships to thrive in the construction industry, it's important to create a broader ecosystem that promotes collaboration. This involves fostering not only the relationships between clients and contractors but also between all parties involved in a project, including consultants, subcontractors, and suppliers.

By building a collaborative ecosystem, stakeholders can create a network of trusted partners who work together across multiple projects, ensuring that each partner's strengths are fully leveraged to achieve the best possible outcomes.

Key components of a collaborative ecosystem Includes:

• Open Communication: Regular and honest communication between all stakeholders is the bedrock of a collaborative ecosystem.

This ensures that everyone is aligned with the project's goals and can address issues as they arise.

• Shared Learning: Each project provides valuable lessons that can benefit future projects. By fostering a culture of continuous learning and knowledge-sharing across the ecosystem, partners can avoid repeating mistakes and improve their processes.

• Joint Innovation: Partners who work together across multiple projects are more likely to innovate together. For example, a contractor and client who have developed a strong working relationship may collaborate on the development of new construction techniques or sustainable practices, benefiting both parties and the broader industry.

Case Study: UAE's Commercial Vehicle Load Regulation

Balancing Safety and Industry Needs In 2023, the UAE Cabinet introduced Resolution No. 138, setting limits on commercial vehicle loads to improve road safety, extend road service life, and support environmental objectives by reducing the carbon footprint of land transport. This regulation capped the weight of commercial vehicles based on axle count, with a maximum load limit of 65 tons.

The government aimed to enhance infrastructure sustainability, reduce traffic accidents, and align with the UAE's broader environmental goals.

However, this regulation encountered notable concerns from stakeholders within the construction and logistics sectors.

Developers voiced concerns that these restrictions would lead to increased transportation costs, potentially escalating project costs and timelines, especially for the large-scale projects that are a hallmark of the Middle Eastern construction landscape. The increased financial burden and logistical constraints could hinder timely project delivery, impacting contractors, suppliers, and clients alike.

In response to these concerns, the UAE Cabinet deferred the implementation of the regulation in early 2024, directing the Ministry of Energy and Infrastructure to conduct further studies. This case exemplifies the complex balancing act between regulatory ambitions and industry needs, especially in sectors like construction, where logistics and transportation costs are significant. This demonstrates the UAE Government's commitment to fostering a supportive business environment and prioritizing measures that minimize potential financial strain for businesses.

This example underscores the importance of collaborative decision-making between government bodies and industry stakeholders. By engaging in open dialogue and conducting further studies, the UAE demonstrates a commitment to finding a balance that advances both safety and efficiency in the construction and logistics sectors.

Conclusion: Long-Term Success Through Collaboration

In an industry that has traditionally been focused on short-term project gains, the construction sector in the Middle East is beginning to recognize the long-term benefits of building lasting relationships.

Contractors, clients, and consultants who prioritize collaboration, transparency, and mutual success are better positioned to succeed in an increasingly competitive and complex marketplace.

As the industry continues to evolve, long-term relationships will become a key differentiator for companies seeking to deliver projects efficiently, sustainably, and with minimal disputes. By focusing on the bigger picture and investing in long-term partnerships, stakeholders can achieve greater stability, financial health, and project success.

In the next chapter, we will explore how collaborative contracts and long-term relationships contribute to increased efficiency and reduced delays, providing examples of how these approaches have already proven successful in other markets.

Chapter 6: Increasing Efficiency, Reducing Delays

In the construction industry, efficiency and time management are critical to project success. Delays can quickly lead to cost overruns, strained relationships, and even legal disputes. In the Middle East, where many large-scale projects are subject to tight deadlines and complex coordination requirements, delays have historically been a significant issue. However, by adopting collaborative contracts and building long-term partnerships, the industry is starting to see improvements in efficiency and reductions in project delays.

How Collaborative Contracts Increase Efficiency

Collaborative contracts provide mechanisms that enhance efficiency by promoting cooperation, open communication, and problem-solving among stakeholders.

When parties work together with aligned incentives, they are more likely to resolve issues quickly, avoid unnecessary disputes, and keep the project on track.

Here are several ways collaborative contracts increase efficiency:

1. Early Issue Resolution: In adversarial contract frameworks, even small issues can escalate into disputes that cause significant delays. Collaborative contracts, on the other hand, are designed to encourage open dialogue and early issue identification. This enables the project team to address potential problems before they become major setbacks.

2. Streamlined Decision-Making: Collaborative contracts often include provisions for joint decision-making, where stakeholders work together to make critical project decisions. This reduces the need for lengthy back-and-forth discussions, speeding up the decision-making process and keeping the project on schedule.

3. Incentives for On-Time Delivery: Many collaborative contracts include performance-based incentives that reward stakeholders for completing projects on time or ahead of schedule. These incentives

align the interests of all parties, encouraging them to work together toward timely completion.

Case Study: The Riyadh Metro Project

The Riyadh Metro, one of the largest infrastructure projects in Saudi Arabia, faced significant complexity and coordination challenges due to its scale. To mitigate delays, the project adopted a collaborative contract approach, with all stakeholders—including contractors, consultants, and government bodies— engaged in joint decision-making and transparent communication.

This collaborative model helped reduce the number of disputes and kept the project on track, even in the face of unexpected challenges. The project's ability to maintain momentum through efficient coordination and early issue resolution has been cited as one of the key reasons for its continued progress.

Resources like RICS provide insights into challenges faced in major Middle Eastern projects, including dispute trends and collaborative strategies that can mitigate these issues.

Reducing Delays Through Effective Communication

Delays in construction projects are often caused by miscommunication or a lack of timely information sharing between stakeholders. In traditional contracts, parties may withhold information to protect their interests, which can lead to misunderstandings and delays in addressing issues.

Collaborative contracts promote transparent communication from the outset. This involves setting clear communication protocols, establishing regular project meetings, and using technology to share information in real-time.

Case Study: The Lusail City Development in Qatar

The Lusail City Development in Qatar, a multibillion-dollar city-building project, adopted a collaborative approach to reduce delays.

Stakeholders utilized advanced communication tools such as Building Information Modeling (BIM) to share real-time data on project progress. BIM allowed contractors, architects, and consultants to visualize potential clashes or delays before they occurred, enabling them to make swift decisions to prevent disruptions.

The use of real-time communication and collaboration tools helped the project avoid many of the delays that typically plague large-scale developments. The ability to identify and resolve issues early, thanks to transparent communication, significantly enhanced the efficiency of the project.

The Role of Flexibility in Reducing Delays

One of the primary challenges of traditional contracts is their rigidity. When unexpected changes occur, these contracts often fail to accommodate flexibility, leading to delays as parties dispute how to handle the changes. Collaborative contracts, by contrast, build flexibility into the contract structure, enabling stakeholders to adapt to changing circumstances more efficiently.

Keyelements of flexibility in collaborative contracts include:

1. Change Management Processes: Collaborative contracts often include clear processes for managing changes to the project scope, schedule, or budget. These processes involve all stakeholders and allow for adjustments to be made quickly without unnecessary disputes or delays.

2. Proactive Problem-Solving: By fostering an environment of trust and collaboration, these contracts encourage parties to take a proactive approach to problem-solving. Instead of waiting for issues to escalate, stakeholders work together to address challenges as soon as they arise.

Case Study: Dubai's Al Maktoum International Airport Expansion

The expansion of Al Maktoum International Airport in Dubai, one of the world's largest airport projects, faced several logistical challenges that required flexibility in project execution.

By adopting collaborative contract principles, the project team was able to quickly adapt to changing requirements, such as design modifications and shifts in passenger traffic forecasts.

The flexibility built into the project's contractual framework allowed the airport expansion to continue without significant delays. Stakeholders engaged in proactive problem-solving, ensuring that any adjustments to the project plan were made efficiently and with minimal disruption.

Human Factors: Ensuring the Right People Are in the Right Roles

While technology, communication, and flexible contracts all play a role in increasing efficiency, it's important not to overlook the human element. Having the right people in critical roles can make the difference between a successful project and one plagued by delays. In many cases, the root of claims or disputes often stems from interpersonal conflicts or individuals allowing ego to influence their actions. Addressing these underlying human factors can prevent escalation and promote smoother collaboration.

In collaborative projects, ensuring that decision-makers are well-equipped to manage risks, communicate effectively, and solve problems is essential.

When the right people are in place, they can drive the project forward efficiently and ensure that any delays are minimized.

Case Study: The Role of Project Leadership in the Burj Khalifa

The construction of the Burj Khalifa, the world's tallest building, required a high level of coordination and expertise. Throughout the project, strong leadership was essential in managing the complexities of building such a unique structure. The project managers and engineers were highly skilled, with the authority to make decisions quickly, which helped avoid delays caused by indecision or miscommunication.

The leadership team's proactive approach to problem-solving, combined with a collaborative contract structure, enabled the Burj Khalifa to be completed on schedule despite the numerous technical challenges it faced.

Conclusion: Collaboration and Flexibility for Efficient Project Delivery

The construction industry in the Middle East faces unique challenges in terms of scale, complexity, and tight deadlines. However, as we've seen through the examples of projects like the Riyadh Metro, Lusail City, and Al Maktoum Airport, adopting collaborative contracts, fostering transparent communication, and building flexibility into projects can significantly enhance efficiency and reduce delays.

By focusing on proactive problem-solving, streamlining decision-making processes, and ensuring the right people are in place, stakeholders can achieve smoother project execution, avoid costly delays, and ultimately deliver better outcomes for all parties involved.

In the final chapter, we will discuss the broader implications of these collaborative practices for the future of the construction industry in the region and how they can help build a more resilient, efficient, and prosperous industry.

Conclusion: Moving Towards a Collaborative Future

The construction industry in the Middle East stands at a pivotal moment. For decades, the industry has been defined by adversarial contracts, rigid frameworks, and a focus on short-term project wins rather than long-term partnerships. These practices, while ingrained in the region, have led to inefficiencies, cost overruns, disputes, and, in some cases, the financial collapse of major contractors. However, the future of the industry lies not in conflict but in collaboration.

As examples from projects like the Riyadh Metro, Lusail City Development, and Al Maktoum International Airport demonstrate, collaborative contracts, transparent communication, and flexible project management approaches are already driving significant improvements in efficiency, cost control, and project outcomes. These successful projects show us a path forward—one where mutual trust, risk-sharing, and long-term partnerships replace adversarial practices.

The Need for Industry-Wide Change

For the construction industry to thrive in the coming years, particularly in the Middle East, where megaprojects are increasingly common, an industry-wide shift toward collaboration is essential. This shift must encompass all stakeholders, from developers and clients to contractors, consultants, and government regulators. Each party has a role to play in driving this transformation:

1. Clients: Must lead by example, embracing contract frameworks that prioritize fairness, risk-sharing, and collaborative problem-solving. Clients must also incentivize long-term partnerships, rewarding contractors for efficiency and innovation rather than penalizing them for unexpected challenges.

2. Contractors: Need to be open to collaboration, actively participating in risk-sharing frameworks and fostering transparent communication with clients. Contractors should also invest in continuous improvement, focusing on enhancing their capabilities in collaborative project

management and early issue resolution.

3. Consultants and Project Managers: Play a critical role in facilitating communication and ensuring that all stakeholders are aligned. By acting as neutral intermediaries, they can help resolve disputes before they escalate and ensure that all parties are working toward the same goals.

4. Government and Regulators: Can support this shift by mandating the use of collaborative contract models for public projects and encouraging the private sector to follow suit. Governments can also promote the adoption of innovative technologies that improve transparency and efficiency.

Case Study: The UAE Government's Role in Construction Transformation

In the UAE, the government has played an active role in collaboration ouraging collaboration across the construction sector. In the lead-up to Expo 2020, the government required many of the projects to adopt collaborative contract models and advanced communication technologies like Building Information Modeling (BIM).

These initiatives, combined with performance-based incentives for contractors, helped ensure the timely and efficient completion of projects, even in the face of unexpected challenges like the COVID-19 pandemic.

The UAE's approach serves as a model for how government intervention and leadership can drive industry-wide change, fostering an environment where collaboration becomes the norm rather than the exception.

Building a More Resilient and Sustainable Industry

The benefits of adopting a collaborative approach are not limited to individual project outcomes. By embracing collaboration, the construction industry in the Middle East can build greater resilience and sustainability in the long term. This is particularly important in a region where economic diversification, urban development, and infrastructure expansion are key drivers of growth.

Key advantages of a more collaborative industry include:

• Financial Stability: Contractors and consultants who operate within collaborative frameworks are less likely to face the financial instability caused by unfair risk allocation. By promoting balanced risk-sharing, the industry can avoid the contractor bankruptcies and liquidations that have plagued the sector in recent years.

• Innovation and Efficiency: Collaboration fosters an environment where stakeholders are incentivized to innovate and improve efficiency. Technologies like BIM, prefabrication, and modular construction can be more easily integrated into projects when all parties are working toward a common goal. These innovations lead to faster project completion, reduced waste, and better cost control.

• Attracting Investment: A collaborative, transparent, and efficient construction industry is more likely to attract international investment.

Investors and developers seek stability, reliability, and predictability in their projects—qualities that are best achieved through long-term partnerships and fair contract frameworks.

• Sustainability and Environmental Responsibility: Collaborative contracts are well-suited to projects that focus on sustainability and environmental responsibility. When stakeholders share the same sustainability goals, they are more likely to work together to implement eco-friendly practices, such as reducing carbon footprints, minimizing material waste, and incorporating renewable energy solutions.

Case Study: Masdar City's Collaborative Approach to Sustainability

Masdar City in Abu Dhabi is an example of how a collaborative approach can drive sustainability in construction. From the outset, the project was designed to be a model of sustainable urban development.

Collaborative contracts were used to align the interests of all stakeholders, ensuring that environmental goals were prioritized throughout the project lifecycle. By working together, contractors, consultants, and developers were able to incorporate cutting-edge technologies, such as solar energy and smart city infrastructure, without sacrificing efficiency or profitability.

This project exemplifies how partnerships with shared objectives can foster innovation while maintaining cost efficiency. Sources like Arcadis and McKinsey discuss the importance of collaboration in achieving sustainability and efficiency, making Masdar a compelling case study for your book on collaborative contracts in construction.

The Road Ahead: Embracing the Future of Construction

The future of the construction industry in the Middle East is bright, but it will require a concerted effort to fully realize the benefits of collaboration. The industry must move beyond its reliance on adversarial practices and embrace the principles of transparency, trust, and mutual success.

By doing so, stakeholders can create a more resilient, efficient, and prosperous industry—one that is capable of meeting the region's ambitious development goals.

As we have seen through the various case studies and real-world examples, collaborative contracts, transparent communication, and long-term partnerships are not just theoretical concepts – they are proven strategies that deliver real results. Projects like the Riyadh Metro, Dubai Expo 2020, and Masdar City demonstrate that when stakeholders work together toward shared goals, the outcomes are superior in every respect: fewer delays, lower costs, and greater innovation.

By adopting these collaborative practices on a wider scale, the Middle East construction industry can lead the way in creating a future where every project is delivered with maximum efficiency, minimum disputes, and shared success for all.

Sample Contracts Clauses for Collabration

Here's a framework and some sample clauses for collaborative contracts I would suggest for consideration:

Pilot Project Selection: Start by piloting collaborative contracts on smaller projects, focusing on mutual trust- building.

Communication Protocol Setup: Define reporting structures, meeting frequency, and digital tools for transparency.

Risk Assessment Meetings: Schedule joint risk assessment sessions at key project phases to adjust risk allocation as needed.

Risk-Sharing Clause: "Both parties agree to a mutual risk-sharing framework, wherein risks related to site conditions, regulatory changes, and unforeseen delays are allocated to the party best positioned to manage them. A joint review panel shall assess risk allocation adjustments at each project milestone."

Transparency and Communication Clause: "All stakeholders shall participate in bi-weekly progress meetings, with open-book accounting to ensure financial transparency. Each party shall provide updates on project-related costs, timelines, and anticipated challenges to enable timely, collaborative solutions."

Incentive Clause for Timely Delivery: "In recognition of the collaborative effort required to complete the project on time, a bonus equivalent to X% of the project cost will be awarded to the contractor if the project is completed within the agreed timeline. Conversely, each party agrees to share penalties if delays are due to shared responsibility."

Final Call to Action: Shaping a Collaborative Future

As a professional in the construction industry, you have the power to drive this change. Whether you are a client, contractor, consultant, or regulator, you can advocate for and implement collaborative practices that prioritize long-term success over short-term gains. By doing so, you will not only contribute to the success of individual projects but also help shape a more sustainable, resilient, and prosperous construction industry for the future.

References

Chapter 1: Breaking Free from Adversarial Contracts

1. Gulf News. "UAE Postpones Heavy Vehicle Weight Limit Rule." *Gulf News*, February 18, 2024. Retrieved from https://www.gulfnews.com
2. RICS. "Global Construction Disputes Report." *Royal Institution of Chartered Surveyors*, 2023. Provides insight into traditional contract disputes and collaborative solutions.

Chapter 2: The Rise of Partnered Contracts

1. McKinsey & Company. "Collaborative Contracting in Construction." *McKinsey Insights*, 2023. Retrieved from https://www.mckinsey.com.
2. World Built Environment Forum, RICS. "Collaborative Contracting in Construction Projects." *World Built Environment Forum*, 2022. Retrieved from https://www.rics.org.

Chapter 3: The Role of Trust and Transparent Communication

1. The Law Reporters. "UAE Defers Law Regulating Heavy Vehicle Dimensions." *The Law Reporters*, February 19, 2024. Retrieved from https://thelawreporters.com
2. HKA. "CRUX Insight Report." *HKA*, 2023. Analysis on common dispute causes and trust-based solutions in Middle Eastern construction.

Chapter 4: Balancing Risk for a Healthier Industry

1. Arcadis. "Global Construction Disputes Report 2023." *Arcadis*, 2023. Covers dispute trends in the Middle East, including effective risk-sharing practices.
2. Gulf Today. "Cabinet Postpones Implementation of Resolution Regulating Weights and Dimensions of Heavy Vehicles in UAE." *Gulf Today*, February 18, 2024. Retrieved from https://www.gulftoday.ae
3. Reed Smith LLP – "Expo 2020 - Managing and Resolving Construction Disputes" https://www.reedsmith.com/en/perspectives/2014/11/expo-2020--part-5-managing-and-resolving-construct
4. Mace Group – "Expo 2020 Dubai: A First for the Middle East" https://www.macegroup.com/projects/expo-2020
5. Mondaq – "Managing and Resolving Construction Disputes for Expo 2020" https://www.mondaq.com/construction-planning/355374/expo-2020--part-5-managing-and-resolving-construction-disputes
6. Gulf News – "Expo 2020 Dubai Project: Progress and Partnerships" https://gulfnews.com/expo-2020/news/dubai-expo-2020-project-progress-so-far-1.1902596

Chapter 5: Building Long-Term Relationships, Not Short-Term Gains

1. HKA. "The Benefits of Long-Term Collaborative Partnerships in Middle Eastern Projects." *HKA Insights*, 2022. Analysis of sustained partnerships in public-sector construction.
2. RICS. "Construction Contracting Practices in the Middle East." *Royal Institution of Chartered Surveyors*, 2021. Discusses the advantages of long-term, collaborative partnerships.

Chapter 6: Increasing Efficiency, Reducing Delays

1. McKinsey & Company. "Efficiency and Collaboration in Major Construction Projects." *McKinsey & Company*, 2023. Retrieved from https://www.mckinsey.com.
2. Gulf News. "Collaborative Frameworks for Mega Projects in the UAE." *Gulf News*, 2023. Examines benefits seen in projects like the Dubai Expo and Riyadh Metro.

General Sources

1. Arcadis. "Middle East Construction Dispute Report." *Arcadis*, 2023. Comprehensive look at dispute causes and resolutions across the region.
2. RICS. "The Importance of Collaborative Contracting in High-Stakes Projects." *Royal Institution of Chartered Surveyors*, 2023. Provides an industry overview of collaborative frameworks and their application in construction.

www.ingramcontent.com/pod-product-compliance
Lightning Source LLC
Chambersburg PA
CBHW041452210326
41599CB00004B/222